SAINT MONICA

Saint Monica

Mary Biddinger

Black Lawrence Press

Black Lawrence Press
www.blacklawrence.com

Executive Editor: Diane Goettel
Book Design: Steven Seighman
Cover: *Saint Gabi* by Amy Freels, copyright 2009. Used with permission.

Black Lawrence Press
115 Center Avenue
Pittsburgh, PA 15215
U.S.A.

Published 2011 by Black Lawrence Press, an imprint of Dzanc Books

First edition May, 2011
ISBN-13: 978-0982876619
Printed in the United States

Contents

Saint Monica

Memorial: 27 August

Mother of Saint Augustine of Hippo, whose writings about her are the primary source of our information. A Christian from birth, she was given in marriage to a bad-tempered adulterous pagan named Patricius. She prayed constantly for the conversion of her husband (who converted on his death bed), and of her son (who converted after a wild life). Spiritual student of Saint Ambrose of Milan. Reformed alcoholic.

Born 322 at Tagaste (Souk Ahrus), Algeria.
Died 387 at Ostia, Italy

Patronage: abuse victims, alcoholics, alcoholism, difficult marriages, disappointing children, homemakers, housewives, married women, mothers, victims of adultery, victims of unfaithfulness, victims of verbal abuse, widows, wives.

~From the *Patron Saints Index* online

For all the girls with names that begin with *M*.

SAINT MONICA OF THE GAUZE

The room is red with iodine. Her ears stop
and her thighs slacken against
the bed. The owls would like to unwrap

her, as owls do, always looking
for the next loose shutter, the goldfinch
bathing in a pile of spilled parmesan

in the convenience store parking lot.
She explains a few things. Static
wracks the telephone line, a dry tornado

on the helipad after a freeway crash.
The linoleum has seen years of other feet
and beds rolling in and out, how

they hauled her from the gurney as if
she weighed something other
than what was left. They ask: but what

about your Cleveland flowering pear
trees, or the creeping vinca, the clematis
your husband promised to burn if it

came back? They say that she will get out.
There will be time and muscle
enough for hanging wet towels on a line.

SAINT MONICA OF THE THAW

No, they would never find her under the ice
like a lost scarf snowed away for months
and replaced. There would be no need to
donate her record collection to the library
or avoid her bedroom window after dusk.
She would never stare up at the rafters
for any other reason than to spot bats
exiting through the base of a ceiling fan.

In fact, she didn't even know the cold,
had to lie when friends asked about her
bare legs under a kilt, the muslin slips
she slept in, her windows always cracked
in January while the rest were huddled,
hot bricks at their toes. When she fell
into the icy river, she climbed right out
on her own, before a teacher and a rope

somersaulted down the crusted ledge.
Monica did not even peel off her coat
before untangling Miss Nells, brushing
the snow from her pin curls, flipping her
skirt back over her knees. How did she
keep quiet about the dingy pantalets, red
garter hidden under all that wool, the way
the rope knotted itself around them both?

SAINT MONICA STAYS THE COURSE

One year at Saint Joseph, the girls who had first names beginning with M were invited to walk in the May Crowning procession. The Blessed Virgin stood at the side of the altar waiting to be topped with vines and lilies of the valley. Sister Cathleen instructed the girls in the correct way to proceed. Everyone had to wear white, of course, and no eyelet lace unless it was lined underneath. No ribbons in colors other than blue, for the Virgin. Monica's mother had stayed up all night stitching an empire-waist smock with puff sleeves that were perky but not bulbous. Sister Cathleen measured hems with a metal ruler beforehand. Sister Cathleen said: whatever happens, do not stop marching. Do not look into the pews to smirk at your best friend or your brother. Keep your eyes on the Virgin. Clasp your bunch of daffodils, but don't clasp it too hard or else the heads will shoot off and distract the other girls. Monica practiced this, the hard enough but not too hard, on a limp feather duster at home. Sister Cathleen instructed: do not stop the procession, whatever happens. If Molly Grace faints on the steps and suffers a concussion upon impact, breaking her glasses, keep marching. If Maeve erupts in her first period like a water balloon tossed on a bed of thumbtacks, keep marching. If Meaghan and Melanie collide in front of the altar, white Mary Janes interlocking, proceed as planned. Magdalena may vomit up her cornflakes once she is seated in the pews. She has done this before. Keep your eyes to yourself. If you fear you may have explosive diarrhea during the ceremony, say two Hail Marys and one Glory Be, and get over it. Monica, if Father places the wreath in your hands, keep your fingers open like a sparrow's wings and do not scuff your shoes as you walk up to the Virgin. Surrender the crown to six-foot-tall Maureen, star of the Lady Irish. Whatever happens, proceed as planned. If your tuition checks are returned due to non-sufficient funds, show up at class anyway, until the Bursar walks you to the front door. If you feel like you will die after ten-hour shifts waiting tables, stray husbands pinching your ass and snapping your bra strap, say two Hail Marys and one Glory Be, and get over it. If your fiancé slams you against a wall and you suffer a concussion upon impact, breaking your glasses, keep marching to the bathroom with a bottle of Windex and a roll of paper towels and make that crooked mirror shine. If he appears above you in the middle of the night, reeking of Wild Turkey and Kools, do not push him away. Proceed as planned. You have done this before.

SAINT MONICA AND THE HATE

Because she didn't live in a trailer. Because
she knew the answer, even before Miss Nells
asked the question, hand darting up as soon
as she heard the words *What year*. Because
she always won the blue ribbon, and often

the red, too. All parents loved her, dropped
her name when scolding about tangled hair,
crooked hems. No wonder her girlfriends
stabbed her in the back with knives, forks,
hairpins, chopsticks, whatever was handy

and sharp. The girls stole a pair of Monica's
Care Bear panties from her dresser, dredged
them in mud, then hung them on the railing
outside school. Caroline told everyone about
the cyst under Monica's left arm, claimed

that Monica wrote all the answers on her
thighs in Karo syrup, fingered the stickiness
to guide her though algebra tests. How could
they know that Monica's mother not only
cut her own tri-color fettuccini by hand,

but counted how many strands that Monica
was allowed? The naked weigh-ins, creak
of the Sharpie marker on the back of her legs.
The boys radiated around her like a bonfire
because they wanted to know if the Tigers

would make it to the Series, or what kind
of fish had stolen off with their favorite lure,
and under which bridge to find it. She was no
threat to the spiral-perm crew, girls jamming
five legs' worth of thigh into acid-washed

mini skirts. Years later, they would hate
Monica for the brilliance of her peonies,
the straightness of her children's bangs.
For the way she *did it all*, and still baked
the best cherry walnut cobbler on the block.

SAINT MONICA AND THE DEVIL'S PLACE

At school they were too polite to call it *Hell*, though she heard the word on her mother's eight-tracks, seeping between damp towels in the bathroom, hovering in the silver of the old hall mirror. Monica knew who went there and why, regardless of time spent fluffing the chrysanthemums outside the rectory. She'd go to the Devil's Place herself if it meant one hour alone with Kevin McMillan in the falling-down barn. Sister Rita said it was hot, but Monica could live with that. Mrs. Dettweiler next door crushed cigarettes out on her daughter's back. She was on her way to the Devil's Place, along with the Simmons twins, and Monica's uncle who thought he could piss out an electrical fire, ended up burning down the Kroger instead. There were, of course, exceptions. If he was mean enough you could take a cinderblock to your husband's head in the middle of the night, as long as you called the police afterwards, produced the notebook of grievances when officers arrived. You could sign your husband up for a war, then dash your face with mauve lipstick on the night they handed him a gun. If you were married to one of the Simmons twins you could toss the car keys down a sewer grate, sprint to JC Penney for a white sale bonanza with the charge card, knowing you'd be safe until Randy or Ricky made it out of the sludge. Monica would not go to the Devil's Place over shoplifted Raisinets or hair gel, but she would sign away her soul for an afternoon swimming with Kevin McMillan in the pond at Raccoon Park, as long as they could both be naked and the water above 55 degrees. Perhaps there was hope for Monica's uncle, provided he sold the Firebird, wheeled the recliner to the curb and found a job. If they ever married, Monica would never touch Kevin McMillan while he read the newspaper in his slippers and flannel boxers, or dig a

17

six-foot, three-and-a-half-inch hole in the backyard while the children planted daffodil bulbs. She would not include the Devil's Place on her college application list, as Rhonda Phillips did the day she broke her sister's arm playing darts. When the Simmons twins winked at her, Monica looked away. When Kevin McMillan winked at her, Monica unbuttoned her shirt, showed the hot pink swimsuit underneath.

SAINT MONICA GIVES IT UP

They say chastity is a gift,
like an extra thumb.
But they have never seen

Kevin McMillan bare
to the waist in an apple tree
as Monica did

one Wednesday afternoon
before dance class.
The bun in her hair nearly

unraveled itself.
All of the birds around her
dipped to the ground

in search of stray fire ants.
Still, she clung
to her Saint Christopher

medal, taped up
more kitten posters in her
school locker,

pounded the bread dough
a little bit harder.
Twenty years later now

and she still sees
him: grinding cross-sections
of a fallen oak, or

staggering across a field to her
in pink moments
before the alarm clock's blare.

SAINT MONICA COMPOSES A FIVE-PARAGRAPH ESSAY ON GIRARD'S THEORY OF TRIANGULAR DESIRE

Two Dominican Sisters and a Schnauzer sit on the back patio in late June, eating deviled eggs and day-old Wonder bread. Years ago the schnauzer would've been plotting a way to kill them both, maybe suffocating them in the collapsible umbrella or going for the throats. But now he's deflated and damp, happy to lick the socket of an egg and blink as heavy bumblebees bomb the petunias.

Molly Grace Simmons, Caroline Delaney, and Brigit McPherson occupied the space under the gym stairs like warlords with thick strawberry lip gloss and transparent glitter nail polish. One day Caroline brought a game to school with her: a maze small enough to fit in a uniform blouse pocket. Every time she patted her breast we imagined the tiny silver ball rattling against the plastic corridors and cardboard backing. When Caroline walked she made the sound of a pebble in the toe of a loafer. The boys imagined their tongues rattling against the corridors of Caroline. Sister Rita confiscated the maze, made Caroline deposit it in the rubbish bin while everyone watched.

Three noteworthy disappointments: Touching a Weimaraner for the first time and realizing that its fur was more like a donkey's than the satin everyone imagined. The eyes were vacant, not all-knowing. Not as frightful as breaking into the abandoned mill at midnight with only a one-inch Bic lighter as protection. The floorboards were slick as strawberry lip gloss and the whole place reeked of eggs and wet dog. But there were no spirits. We left and hiked to the White Hen without really understanding why. The cashier asked for identification, so we had to surrender our six pack of tropical wine coolers and tin of Skoal. We stood in the rain and then went home.

When three distant lights converge into one, the lost sailors know they can enter the harbor. If Kevin McMillan raps three times on the garage door, shimmy down the ladder and let him in. Every third container is subject to a rigorous six-point test, which only means marking one extra box on the roster for every three hundred that pass by. Kevin can easily be hidden in a crawlspace or even behind a door that isn't opened or closed very frequently. Remind him to stay completely silent and not to breathe.

When Jason and Kevin shake hands are they really touching each other, or the person they have both touched in rooms striated by horizontal blinds? When they look into each other's eyes is there anything between them other than a set of Acuvue contact lenses? Mixing Skoal and tropical wine coolers can result in double, even triple vision. The best way to break into an abandoned mill is to devise a cheerleading pyramid: two biggest people on the bottom and the smallest on top to pry open windows. Following that, everyone slips in. It's mimetic. It's the ship's wheel held by both sailors at once, looking at their hands instead of the rain.

SAINT MONICA'S SWEET SIXTEEN

It begins with a fistfight:
her boyfriend and uncle Paul

shoving each other during
an episode of Punky Brewster,

her favorite show, television
decorated with pink ribbons,

the girls from school bug-
eyed and silent. Monica

wishes she had a hammer
to throw through the window.

The mini-cupcakes scatter
like fleas on a cat's back

and warm Kool Aid churns
inside the Waterford bowl.

Behind green foyer drapes,
Amelia Fletcher loses her

virginity and it only takes
twenty seconds, no love-

blisters, copper belt buckles,
whiskey, or dramatic cello

solos in the background.
Amelia returns to the group

a petunia after the first frost,
slightly rumpled, transparent.

Monica's mother arrives
to serve rigatoni with garlic

and pine nuts. Paul and Jason
collapse together onto the sofa,

locked and jabbing, shattering
the glass coffee table, Lladro

figurine of a girl lathering
a dog in a bathtub. Monica

retreats to her special place
under the stairs, her stuffed

owl, yearbook and flashlight
tucked into a nylon backpack.

It takes her seven minutes
to realize that she is not alone.

SAINT MONICA KEEPS IT STRAIGHT

Monica's diorama of Niagara Falls did not win first place at the geography fair. Her horse got spooked by a broom and threw her before the big jump. She did not get the role of Wendy in Peter Pan, or even second understudy. The science experiment involving large quantities of cadmium, the toothpick hotel that dissolved in rain at the bus stop, even the piglets she groomed with her own hairbrush—all failures. But on scoliosis screening day Monica wore her red turtleneck under a uniform jumper. She polished her shoes the night before and the morning of, even though she wouldn't be wearing shoes. She wouldn't be wearing anything but her gym shorts and bra, the one glorious day that she was at the head of her class. Between screenings—always in January—everyone forgot that Monica had the largest breasts at Saint Joseph. It was easy to overlook the fact. She never wore the skirt and blouse, which required double-stick tape to keep shut if you were anywhere near puberty. Her grandmother had even stitched a discreet Lucite snap into the space between the buttons, but to no avail. The snap burst the minute Monica's hand shot up to answer the question: *What is the most common impurity in zinc, and is it deadly? If so, how deadly?* For the rest of the day she had to hold that keyhole shut while balancing her lunch tray, scribbling notes to Kevin McMillan, writing poetry about Kevin McMillan, sketching the likeness of Kevin McMillan gently on her thigh, passing the spelling tests up to Sister Rita, scanning Kevin McMillan's paper and recoiling at his butchery of the word *jocular*. It wasn't that Monica was obsessed with her posture, or sure that her spinal column would never curve into an S or a C. Sister Joan didn't even lift her bra strap as she did with some of the other girls. Monica almost wished she'd take her time, a dramatic glance at the duct tape line on the gym wall as the other girls gaped. A raised eyebrow, or a scurry to the medical guide. Instead Monica was waved right through, even as she superimposed Kevin McMillan's face onto Sister Joan's, imagined the two of them tearing out of the school parking lot in a gold Camaro. The girls who passed the screening dribbled basketballs at the other end of the gym, but Monica was halfway down M-20 with snowflakes like sequins on her 18-hour front closure Maidenform, Kevin at the wheel with a copy of Vonnegut in his pocket, the poplar trees all scandalized and clapping.

SAINT MONICA GETS HER MAN

The girls in long skirts are the slowest
to get away, on bicycle or foot,
over fences and through mud ditches.

The ones with thick stockings fall first,
snag their blouses, turn back
for a last look before the burning

windmill implodes. She was always
smarter than that. When her
stepfather lowered himself into

the cellar, Monica was ready: a jar
of pickled eggs and an awl.
When the boys under the bridge

stopped her, she didn't stop, only
poured a handful of gravel
from her sleeve, went on walking

toward a stand of elms and phlox.
The woman who picks out
a new red lipstick at Woolworths

always turns up in somebody's
storm sewer by nightfall,
wrapped in a blood-soaked sheet.

There's a rule to it, like the plaits
her mother stitched to her
skin to make them stay in place.

SAINT MONICA HEARS *FREEBIRD*
FOR THE FIRST TIME

in a bombed out fruit stand off M-20,
where the boys heat pellets of crack
in hamburger foil, the girls unsnap

their bras under sweaters and lean
like melting snow banks pocked
with salt. A school bus backfires

black soot into the woods. One girl
pulls a cellophane-wrapped cupcake
from her pocket, then drop kicks it

until the others join in, stomping.
A paint-spattered radio leaks out
of Jason's duffel bag, and Monica

can't move her moon boots fast
enough to unzip the bag, sweep oak
leaves away from the single speaker.

At first she thinks it is Prokofiev
or the sound of an icicle plunging
into a lake. Then it is a woman

crouched over a gas station toilet,
retching. Two bums pummeling
each other with lumber outside

the Hallmark store. A coyote
at the heels of a jackrabbit
and the crush of blood, string

set to trip anyone who passes,
the smell of butane and ammonia,
shadow of shoulders and wrists.

SAINT MONICA TAKES COMMUNION TWICE

The first time it was the girl with hair tucked behind her ears. The second time it was the girl with hair in her face, hands unfolded, bra strap peeking out from the neckline of her sweater. She just got back in line and did it all over again. The funny thing was that nobody even noticed, as if those same cordovan Hush Puppies hadn't just passed the altar and scuffed the floor in front of the choir, leaving a flesh-colored ribbon of rubber. Was she really that anonymous? When Monica reached the rear of the church she stepped back into line for the long walk down the aisle, like a widow ready to do it all over again and hoping there would be more sex this time. Monica didn't feel any more satisfied. Each trip was separate to her, and unrelated. Nobody dared her to do it. Years later the girl with hair tucked behind her ears would be taking notes on Shakespeare's Sonnet 144 while the girl with hair in her face stared (behind the hair) at Kevin McMillan, then ditched at break and spent the second half of class in the janitor's closet with dreadlocked mops and ghosty bottles of ammonia, Kevin McMillan half naked in front of her, the two of them blowing cigarette smoke out the ventilation grate and drinking water from a rubber hose. The girl with hair tucked behind her ears took two or three showers a day. Her boyfriend Jason took four and shaved twice, even though he didn't need to. They went on dates to museums of natural history and daylily farms, or spent weekends carving pumpkins and swimming laps for diabetes research. Monica and Jason had a collective dream involving a Golden Retriever named Pfeffernusse and a silver Volkswagen hatchback. The girl with hair tucked behind her ears called in to work with strep throat and everyone signed a card for her. The girl with the hair in her face left a voicemail at 4:26 am—

something about a lost filling or a flat tire—and spent the day chain smoking in Kevin McMillan's childhood bedroom where he moved after flunking out and getting divorced. His parents still had his engraved wedding clock on their mantelpiece. The girl with hair in her face remembered this detail while clutching the mahogany headboard of his parents' bed as he nailed her from behind, or when she slipped off his mother's cantaloupe silk nightgown and folded it back into the nightstand drawer. The girl with hair behind her ears slept in flannel boxers and a Hard Rock Café sweatshirt. Would both girls meet somewhere in the future, standing next to each other in a Denny's bathroom? The girl with the hair in her face showing up for a job interview (still smelling like Captain Morgan's) in lint-flecked yoga pants, only to be escorted into the office of the girl with hair tucked behind her ears, cross and judgmental, revving the paper shredder. Both girls might land parts as extras in a film, but then kaboom, they'd be discovered by the same director at the same time and drafted to star opposite each other in a mini-series. Or could it be some Sunday in Ordinary Time, the Eucharistic minister with hair tucked behind her ears, the Monica with hair in her face taking that long walk down the aisle, destined to turn around and do it all over again.

SAINT MONICA AT THE OAKLEAF SUITES

Somewhere she heard: *kiss all four walls*
if you want to return. She won't be kissing

any of these walls tonight, or stroking the side
of the bathtub like a child's sweaty forehead.

She once dated a man who checked in,
duct-taped the shower cap over his face

after eating an entire ham on a paper plate,
the Clio motel room rented for three hours.

As a teenager she slept propped in a tub
while her best friend snored into linoleum,

the daybreak wake up call, recital of lies
when parents asked about the junior prom.

Tonight she's the older sister with a charge
card and the girl waiting in the backseat

of the Thunderbird, her date down the hall
with the ice bucket and hitchhiking upstate

in search of mean weed at the same time,
both Stan and Brad, in certain light a Gary

until his shirt comes off and tattoos are gone.
She is the station wagon cruising 32 in a 55,

the next minute driving a Ginsu Bakelite
into the table saying *don't forget to breathe*

when the lights go out. She collects magnetic
key cards in her photo album, crushes the tiny

Dove soap with her heel. She'll be on top
if she isn't already on the bottom.

·

SAINT MONICA OF THE WOODS

Who else but Monica to help them
find the bones? It had been ten years
since they'd spoken. The officer planted

Vanessa's fluorescent pink earring
in one hand, snagged pair of fishnets
in the other. People shifted in their boots.

They would only remember Vanessa
by the way her husband cut her
ear to ear, the hundred wrappers left

beneath the seats of her Thunderbird,
three ghostly daughters who lingered
at the donut counter without ordering.

Years earlier, Vanessa had streaked
Monica's hair with hydrogen peroxide
on cotton balls, layered close to her scalp

under plastic wrap. Vanessa told Monica
the exact way a tampon slides inside, how to
slip your tongue into a boy's mouth,

or tuck the hem of a shirt up through
a v-neck collar, then stalk the fairground
parking lot like a city girl in heat.

They circled the neon roller rink
hand-in-hand, Vanessa sneaking off
to the locker room, even though its stalls

had no doors. She was the kind of girl
who would walk out of the house
without shoes, and not notice for a mile.

In the woods, snow piled up before
the dogs could drop snouts to the grass.
The cops didn't cover Vanessa, frost

filigreed like the see-through nightie
she once shoplifted from JC Penney.
The *Sentinel* would not say she had

a heart of gold, or note that Vanessa's
skin had never splotched or wrinkled, even
when they zipped her into the bag.

SAINT MONICA BURNS IT DOWN

It wasn't her house, but she would strip
it of its bricks if she could, imagining
all of the hair and sesame oil and lye
inside after she had finished. Rooms

where he slipped from pilled flannel
sheets to creep back into her window
with a warm Budweiser in each pocket,
as if he'd never even left. His two terriers

sputtering like motorbike engines through
the night, quiet in his absence, holed up
in ruts beneath the shed. She heard his
feet on the mulch outside, reflections

of his white undershirt illuminating
the window frame. He did not know
there were glass shavings on the ledge,
seeds from the Habanero she coaxed into

unimaginable lengths and heat. When he
landed in the holly bushes he was blind.
Across town, the other woman sipped
cordial by the light of a gas stove.

SAINT MONICA AND THE ITCH

Used to be she only had eyes for the uncles, for the fifteen years older, the stiff dark jeans her girlfriends would giggle at, the men in t-shirts reading *Moustache Rides 5¢*, confusing Monica because they were clean shaven. The boys in her class were doughy and pimpled, always lurching into her in the hall and dropping their pencils. At the county fair Monica lingered in the horse barn, her sandals gathering quills of straw. It was the way Jeff Spatz flicked manure out of a hoof while lighting a cigarette in the other hand, his four white-haired sons stabbing each other with miniature American flags, wife giving the evil eye over a funnel cake. It was Brigit McPherson's neighbor with the motorboat, a six-pack in the cooler, the way his hands moved under her swimsuit and up the back of her neck, *You hold on like this*—she'd never gone water skiing before—*It's like this*—Brigit draped in her Looney Tunes beach towel—*That's it, good girl.* They drove exotic cars, like Mazdas, had a ziplock of weed stashed in the glove box or a joint already rolled and tucked into a pocket. They had tan lines around their wedding rings, worked jobs in air conditioner repair or tool and die, wore terrycloth headbands in summer and mowed the lawn shirtless, claimed a latex allergy but not to worry, they knew what to do. After all, they were twenty-nine or thirty-four, shift managers or certified welders, checked themselves into hotels as Mr. Hanson or Mr. Stan Rusk. Monica's homecoming date was mistaken for a chaperone—they even gave him a clipboard and flashlight for peering under the bleachers—until the principal got wise and called the police. She was left with boys taking bets on how many snickerdoodles they could stuff into their mouths at once, a good Tesla song wasted. Eighteen years later she would dream her way back into that gymnasium, while Randy from next door trimmed the hedges. Jason was out of town on business. The children pressed their noses to the screen, watching each thwack to the arborvitae. Randy wore a t-shirt with *FINISH WHAT YOU STARTED* on the back. Monica wondered what was on the front and offered him some lemonade, only he didn't hear her. He was wearing the tiny headphones that fit inside your ears. Randy was nineteen and had just dropped out of college, come home with a four-inch tattoo on his left calf: a skull with a snake winding through the eye socket. What was it about the way sweat lingered on his collarbone, his hand uncallused as he reached for the lemonade when she asked a second time? Through the lens of the glass tumbler he was backlit like a dashboard, and Monica's face blurred into the aluminum siding. She was thirty-five and knew just what to do. The shrubs shook their goldfinches onto the driveway, and a thunderhead framed the steeple at St. Paul's. Later she would stand an extra minute at the curb, run her fingers along the flagstones as if they were covered with skin.

SAINT MONICA AND THE BABE

Monica's steps are automatic. Her son
twists around in the stroller,
holding one hand out as if to touch
her cheek. He's the Infant Jesus
of Prague, only dressed in
a red onesie and plaid overalls.
Since the day he was born he was never
quite real. Monica keeps him in
her bed at night, won't share him
with the crib rails or midnight creaks.
She wonders if she should pray to him,
ask him questions nobody could answer.

Her daughter studies a dry splotch
of bird shit on the sidewalk. *It's the shape
of a C!* Monica tells her to move along.
People always called Monica an old
soul, wondered why she knew how
to change the blown out fuses, predict
the moment water would kick
into a boil. When the dog had an itch
Monica's hand went right to the tick.

Sometimes at earliest dawn
the baby wakes her with phrases
he can't possibly know. *It's the wind,*
Jason says, *There's no way.*
Is the correct answer to a word
ever another word, or is it a cool palm

on the forehead, a half-hush,
fingers through sweat-curled hair?
The baby wailed during his christening,
but that was just the fear
of candles, the heavy oils Monica
was too afraid to wipe off right away.

SAINT MONICA WISHES ON THE WRONG STAR

Maybe they were both the wrong star.
Perhaps she had wished on a battered
sloop instead of a majestic ocean liner,
read the green tea leaves upside down,
or failed to reveal the correct details
outside the psychic's booth at the fair.

She was always waiting to cut herself,
like in that movie where the protagonist
cut herself. Monica wanted to go in
reverse, even in fourth grade, when she
jammed her legs into last year's yellow
fleece pajamas. The movie's protagonist

washed dishes at the local pub, impaling
pint glasses on the scrub brush panel
two at a time. Monica remembered the best
parts of all her past jobs, especially ones
she despised. The twenty-minute lunch
in the break room with an orange booth,

ashtray overflowing its stale Virginia
Slims. She was reading an Anne Tyler
novel, which almost made it romantic.
The protagonist of the film had probably
wished on the wrong star, which would
explain the two men on opposite sides

of the jukebox. Monica's grandmother
claimed she'd learned to walk backwards
before ever running forward. As a teen
Monica had scoured the previous year's
fashion magazines. Who could blame
her, though? They lived in Michigan,

where nothing ever changed. But when
would the pint glass shatter in her hand,
just like the woman on the screen, limp
ponytail snaking around her shoulders?
Would she have to wait for the flush
of blood, or would the transformation

be instantaneous? The black and white
world reversed, a bite of tea cake spit
out, onto the saucer. How long until
she went back fifteen years, days before
she staked all her money on the wrong
horse, grazing in the wrong pasture.

Acknowledgments

Grateful acknowledgment is made to the editors of the following magazines in which these poems first appeared, sometimes in slightly different versions.

Caffeine Destiny: Saint Monica of the Thaw
The Laurel Review: Saint Monica and the Itch
Ninth Letter: Saint Monica Stays the Course
/nor: Saint Monica and the Devil's Place
North American Review: Saint Monica Gives It Up
Third Coast: Saint Monica Composes a Five Paragraph Essay on
    Girard's Theory of Triangular Desire
Valparaiso Poetry Review: Saint Monica Burns it Down
Whiskey Island Magazine: Saint Monica's Sweet Sixteen
Wicked Alice: Saint Monica of the Gauze

This work would not have been possible without two Individual Excellence Awards from the Ohio Arts Council.

My sincere gratitude to the friends and colleagues who helped me navigate through this project, and who supported me along the way: Nin Andrews, Sandra Beasley, Rachel Dacus, Oliver de la Paz, Thomas Dukes, Michael Dumanis, Justin Evans, Jeannine Hall Gailey, John Gallaher, Susan Grimm, Matthew Guenette, Steve Kistulentz, Erika Meitner, Aimee Nezhukumatathil, Bob Pope, Jay Robinson, Jessica Schantz, Amy Bracken Sparks, and Eric Wasserman. Thank you to Nick Sturm and Mike Krutel for their heroic assistance in times of frenzy.

Many thanks to Black Lawrence Press and Dzanc Books, especially to Diane Goettel. Much appreciation to Amy Freels for the stunning cover image and for her incredible friendship. Love and eternal thankfulness to my parents, and to Eric, Gabi, and Ray.

Mary Biddinger is the author of *Prairie Fever* (Steel Toe Books, 2007), and *O Holy Insurgency* (Black Lawrence Press, 2012), and co-editor of one volume of criticism: *The Monkey and the Wrench: Essays into Contemporary Poetics* (U Akron Press, 2011). She edits *Barn Owl Review*, the Akron Series in Poetry, and the Akron Series in Contemporary Poetics, and teaches literature and creative writing at the University of Akron and the NEOMFA program.